Mont

MOTTO:

Watch well.

CREST:

A woman holding an anchor in her right
hand and the head of a savage in her left.

TERRITORY:

Renfrewshire and Ayrshire.

Echoes of a far distant past
can still be found in most names

Montgomery

by Iain Gray

Lang**Syne**
PUBLISHING
WRITING *to* REMEMBER

Lang**Syne**

PUBLISHING

WRITING *to* REMEMBER

79 Main Street, Newtongrange,
Midlothian EH22 4NA
Tel: 0131 344 0414   Fax: 0845 075 6085
E-mail: info@lang-syne.co.uk
www.langsyneshop.co.uk

Design by Dorothy Meikle
Printed by Printwell Ltd
© Lang Syne Publishers Ltd 2016

ISBN 978-1-85217-230-5

Chapter one:

Origins of Scottish surnames

by George Forbes

It all began with the Normans.

For it was they who introduced surnames into common usage more than a thousand years ago, initially based on the title of their estates, local villages and chateaux in France to distinguish and identify these landholdings, usually acquired at the point of a bloodstained sword.

Such grand descriptions also helped enhance the prestige of these arrogant warlords and generally glorify their lofty positions high above the humble serfs slaving away below in the pecking order who only had single names, often with Biblical connotations as in Pierre and Jacques.

The only descriptive distinctions among this peasantry concerned their occupations, like Pierre the swineherd or Jacques the ferryman.

The Normans themselves were originally Vikings (or Northmen) who raided, colonised and eventually settled down around the French coastline.

They had sailed up the Seine in their long-boats in 900AD under their ferocious leader Rollo and ruled the roost in north east France before sailing over to conquer England, bringing their relatively new tradition of having surnames with them.

It took another hundred years for the Normans to percolate northwards and surnames did not begin to appear in Scotland until the thirteenth century.

These adventurous knights brought an aura of chivalry with them and it was said no damsel of any distinction would marry a man unless he had at least two names.

The family names included that of Scotland's great hero Robert De Brus and his compatriots were warriors from families like the De Morevils, De Umphravils, De Berkelais, De Quincis, De Viponts and De Vaux.

As the knights settled the boundaries of

their vast estates, they took territorial names, as in Hamilton, Moray, Crawford, Cunningham, Dunbar, Ross, Wemyss, Dundas, Galloway, Renfrew, Greenhill, Hazelwood, Sandylands and Church-hill.

Other names, though not with any obvious geographical or topographical features, nevertheless derived from ancient parishes like Douglas, Forbes, Dalyell and Guthrie.

Other surnames were coined in connection with occupations, castles or legendary deeds. Stuart originated in the word steward, a prestigious post which was an integral part of any large medieval household. The same applied to Cooks, Chamberlains, Constables and Porters.

Borders towns and forts – needed in areas like the Debateable Lands which were constantly fought over by feuding local families – had their own distinctive names; and it was often from them that the resident groups took their communal titles, as in the Grahams of Annandale, the Elliots and Armstrongs of the East Marches, the Scotts and Kerrs of Teviotdale and Eskdale.

Even physical attributes crept into surnames, as in Small, Little and More (the latter being 'beg' in Gaelic), Long or Lang, Stark, Stout, Strong or Strang and even Jolly.

Mieklejohns would have had the strength of several men, while Littlejohn was named after the legendary sidekick of Robin Hood.

Colours got into the act with Black, White, Grey, Brown and Green (Red developed into Reid, Ruddy or Ruddiman). Blue was rare and nobody ever wanted to be associated with yellow.

Pompous worthies took the name Wiseman, Goodman and Goodall.

Words intimating the sons of leading figures were soon affiliated into the language as in Johnson, Adamson, Richardson and Thomson, while the Norman equivalent of Fitz (from the French-Latin 'filius' meaning 'son') cropped up in Fitzmaurice and Fitzgerald.

The prefix 'Mac' was 'son of' in Gaelic and clans often originated with occupations – as in MacNab being sons of the Abbot, MacPherson and MacVicar being sons of the minister and MacIntosh being sons of the chief.

The church's influence could be found in the names Kirk, Clerk, Clarke, Bishop, Friar and Monk. Proctor came from a church official, Singer and Sangster from choristers, Gilchrist and Gillies from Christ's servant, Mitchell, Gilmory and Gilmour from servants of St Michael and Mary, Malcolm from a servant of Columba and Gillespie from a bishop's servant.

The rudimentary medical profession was represented by Barber (a trade which also once included dentistry and surgery) as well as Leech or Leitch.

Businessmen produced Merchants, Mercers, Monypennies, Chapmans, Sellers and Scales, while down at the old village watermill the names that cropped up included Miller, Walker and Fuller.

Other self explanatory trades included Coopers, Brands, Barkers, Tanners, Skinners, Brewsters and Brewers, Tailors, Saddlers, Wrights, Cartwrights, Smiths, Harpers, Joiners, Sawyers, Masons and Plumbers.

Even the scenery was utilised as in Craig, Moor, Hill, Glen, Wood and Forrest.

Rank, whether high or low, took its place with Laird, Barron, Knight, Tennant, Farmer, Husband, Granger, Grieve, Shepherd, Shearer and Fletcher.

The hunt and the chase supplied Hunter, Falconer, Fowler, Fox, Forrester, Archer and Spearman.

The renowned medieval historian Froissart, who eulogised about the romantic deeds of chivalry (and who condemned Scotland as being a poverty stricken wasteland), once sniffily dismissed the peasantry of his native France as the jacquerie (or the jacques-without-names) but it was these same humble folk who ended up over-throwing the arrogant aristocracy.

In the olden days, only the blueblooded knights of antiquity were entitled to full, proper names, both Christian and surnames, but with the passing of time and a more egalitarian, less feudal atmosphere, more respectful and worthy titles spread throughout the populace as a whole.

Echoes of a far distant past can still be found in most names and they can be borne with pride in commemoration of past generations who fought and toiled in some capacity or other to make our nation what it now is, for good or ill.

Chapter two:

Knightly valour

A powerful family of Norman nobles were the original bearers of what became the proud name of Montgomery and they, in turn, are believed to have taken their name from a Roman commander by the name of Gomericus who held lands in Gaul, now present day France.

Gomericus had given his name to the lands in Calvados, in Normandy, and for centuries the ancestors of today's Montgomerys held the castle of Saint Foy de Montgomery, at Lisieux.

From these roots in the soil of Normandy, the Montgomerys were to flourish in later centuries in England, Wales, and Scotland, owning vast tracts of land and the recipients of a glittering array of honours and titles.

A Roger de Mundegumrie, whose mother was a distant relation of William, Duke of Normandy, accompanied him on his conquest of England in 1066, and was in the thick of the bloody combat at the battle of Hastings.

This battle-hardened warrior was rewarded with not only the lands of Chichester and Arundel, but also the earldom of Arundel.

Not content to rest on his well-deserved laurels, however, he was also at the forefront of the Norman invasion of Wales, capturing Baldwin Castle.

So significant was his impact on Wales, that both a Welsh town and county still bear his name.

During the reign from 1124 until 1153 of Scotland's David I, who had spent a period of his life at the English Court, a number of Anglo-Normans were invited to settle in Scotland.

Among them was a Robert Montgomery, who obtained lands at Eaglesham, in Renfrewshire.

Further lands and honours were to follow over succeeding centuries as the Montgomerys played a leading role in their adopted nation's frequently turbulent affairs.

It should be pointed out that the spelling of the name varies between 'Montgomery' and 'Montgomerie', but for the sake of clarity the more common form of 'Montgomery' is the one adopted for the purposes of this brief historical narrative of the family's colourful lives and times.

One of the earliest Montgomerys to feature in Scotland's roll of battle honours was Sir John Montgomery, 7th Baron of Eaglesham, who was one of the heroes of the battle of Otterburn, in Northumberland, on August 19, 1388.

The Scots had earlier been involved in a skirmish outside the walls of Newcastle when the Scottish commander, James, the 2nd Earl of Douglas, managed to snatch the silk pennant from the lance of his adversary Henry Percy, heir to the 1st Earl of Northumberland and better known to posterity as Henry Hotspur.

Douglas proceeded to lead his army back towards Scotland, but Hotspur, stung by the insult to his honour, swore his precious pennant would never be allowed to cross the border.

He pursued Douglas, and the two armies clashed at Otterburn, the young earl receiving a fatal blow.

As the Scots army faltered, demoralised over the fate of their commander, the famed Banner of the Bloody Heart of the Douglases was raised, however, and this rallied the Scots to victory.

Crucial to the victory was the capture of Hotspur by Sir John Montgomery after the two had engaged in fierce hand-to-hand combat, with an exhausted and blood-spattered Montgomery at last emerging the victor.

The famous duel is recalled in *The Ballad of Chevy Chase*, which describes how the two knights 'swiped swords' and blood flew from their injuries.

In keeping with the chivalric code of the time, high-ranking prisoners such as Hotspur were ransomed for vast sums of money, and the ransom Montgomery received for his defeated foe allowed him to build Polnoon Castle, at Eaglesham.

Later, through a marriage to the heiress of

Sir Hugh Eglinton he acquired the baronies of Eglinton and Ardrossan, in Ayrshire.

To this day, the Montgomery connections with the conservation village of Eaglesham, situated on the southern outskirts of Glasgow, are recalled in the form of street names and a local hotel.

An example of the Montgomerys' selfless actions on behalf of the Scottish Crown came in 1424 when Sir John Montgomery of Ardrossan was one of the sons of the Scottish nobility who was taken as a hostage to England to secure the release from captivity of James I.

James had become a pawn in a struggle between powerful nobles and his father Robert III, culminating in him being carried for his own safety to the refuge of the Bass Rock, in the Firth of Forth.

He stayed here for about a month before a merchant vessel picked him up in March of 1406 to take him to more secure refuge in France, but English pirates captured the ship off Flamborough Head, and the eleven-year-old prince was taken into the custody of England's Henry V.

Robert III died only a few weeks later, and the young prince now became James I of Scotland.

He was not released from custody until the signing of the Treaty of London of December of 1423, which made arrangements that he would be released only for a ransom of £40,000, payable over six years, while twenty-one sons of the Scottish nobility were to be taken as hostages until the full amount was paid.

Sir John Montgomery was one of these hostages who sacrificed his own freedom in the service of his king.

One of his sons, Sir Alexander Irvine, later became a trusted ambassador of the Crown, and was rewarded for his service when he was created Lord Montgomery in about 1449.

The Montgomerys became caught up in a bitter power struggle when a group of influential nobles rebelled against James III in favour of his son and heir, the future James IV.

The Montgomerys took the side of the young prince, and fought against the king and his supporters at the battle of Sauchieburn, near Stirling, in June of 1488; fleeing the battlefield, a defeated James III was later mysteriously stabbed to death.

As reward for his support, Hugh, the 3rd Lord Montgomery was rewarded with a grant of Arran, off the Ayrshire coast, and the custodianship of the island's Brodick Castle.

In September of 1513, Lord Montgomery, who had been created Earl of Eglinton in about 1507, was one of the few to escape the terrible slaughter of the battle of Flodden, that claimed the lives of 5,000 Scots including James IV, an archbishop, two bishops, eleven earls, fifteen barons, and 300 knights.

The Scottish monarch had embarked on the venture after Queen Anne of France, under the terms of the Auld Alliance between Scotland and her nation, appealed to him to 'break a lance' on her behalf and act as her chosen knight.

Crossing the border into England at the

head of a 25,000-strong army that included 7,500 clansmen and their kinsmen, James IV had engaged a 20,000-strong force commanded by the Earl of Surrey – but despite their numerical superiority and bravery they proved no match for the skilled English artillery and superior military tactics of Surrey.

Chapter three:

Feuds and vendettas

The Montgomerys served not only the interests of the Scottish Crown but also the French Crown, and this was through the Auld Alliance between the two nations, first forged by treaty in 1295.

In later years a Scots Company served with distinction in the ranks of the French Army.

In 1425, in recognition of the company's valour at the bloody battle against the English at Verneuil one year earlier, an elite unit was raised to serve as a permanent bodyguard to the French monarch.

Divided into both the King's Guard and the King's Bodyguard, the units were collectively known as the Scots Guard.

Granted great privileges and honours, the prestigious guard was composed of the sons of some of the noblest houses in Scotland, such as those of Montgomery, Hay, Sinclair, Hamilton,

Stuart, Seton, Cunningham, and Cockburn. They acted not only as soldiers and bodyguards, but also as courtiers and diplomats.

Three members of the guard would stand on either side of the enthroned French monarch at state ceremonies, while guardsmen also slept in the royal bedchamber.

In 1559 the captain of the Scots Guard was 29-year-old Count Gabriel Montgomery, and in July of that year he became involved in an incident that sent shockwaves throughout Europe.

A great devotee of jousting, the French monarch Henry II had arranged a gala tournament in celebration of a peace treaty with the Hapsburgs of Austria and the marriage of two of his daughters.

Held in Paris, the gala tournament had attracted the cream of European royalty and a glittering retinue of nobles - and all had gone well until Henry insisted on entering the lists himself.

He tilted against both the Duke of Savoy and Francis, Duke of Guise, before competing against his trusted Captain of the Scots Guard.

Both men successfully clashed and splintered lances against one another's shields but, in contravention of the normal rules of the joust, arranged for another contest.

A sliver of wood from Montgomery's shattered lance, however, pierced the king through the right eye, entering the brain, and he died in agony several days later – but not before absolving Montgomery from any blame.

Montgomery nevertheless resigned from his post of captain of the Scots Guard and some time later converted from Catholicism to Protestantism.

He narrowly escaped the slaughter of what became known as the Massacre of St Bartholomew's Day, on August 24, 1572, when thousands of Protestant Huguenots in Paris and the surrounding countryside were hunted down and killed by rampaging Catholic mobs.

Montgomery escaped by swimming the Seine and found refuge in England later returning to France as a leading Protestant commander in the bloody Wars of Religion.

He was betrayed and captured, however, and executed in 1574.

Hugh, the 3rd Earl of Eglinton, was a loyal supporter of the ill-starred Mary, Queen of Scots, and was among the nine earls, nine bishops, 18 lairds and others who signed a bond declaring their support.

The queen had been forced to abdicate and imprisoned in Lochleven Castle, but following her escape her supporters rallied and met her foes, known as the Confederate Lords, at Langside, to the south of Glasgow, on May 13, 1568.

Her forces, under the command of the Earl of Argyll, had been en route to the mighty bastion of Dumbarton Castle, atop its near inaccessible eminence on Dumbarton Rock, on the Clyde, when it was intercepted by a numerically inferior but tactically superior force led by her half-brother, the Earl of Moray.

Cannon fire had been exchanged between both sides before a force of Argyll's infantry tried to force a passage through to the village of Langside, but they were fired on by a disciplined body of musketeers and forced to retreat as Moray launched a cavalry charge on their confused ranks.

The battle proved disastrous for Mary and signalled the death knell of her cause, with more than 100 of her supporters killed or captured and Mary forced to flee into what she then naively thought would be the protection of England's Queen Elizabeth.

The Earl of Eglinton was among those captured and imprisoned. Declared guilty of treason, he finally accepted the rule of Mary's son and successor, James VI.

A bloody feud that for more than two centuries had blighted the lives of the Montgomerys and their Ayrshire neighbours, the Cunninghams, plunged to new depths in the spring of 1586 when the young Hugh, 4th Earl of Eglinton was murdered.

His murder, however, only served to further inflame the hatred between the two families, to the extent that the vendetta did not reach its exhausted conclusion until 75 years later, in 1661.

The spark that lit the flame of this vendetta came in 1448 when Sir Alexander Montgomery, a brother-in-law of Sir Robert Cunningham, was controversially made bailie of Cunningham, a lucrative sinecure that the Cunninghams had held for a number of years and claimed belonged to them by right.

Ten years later, in 1458, the bailieship was restored to the Cunninghams and the feud between the two families intensified.

The Montgomerys burned down the Cunningham stronghold of Kerelaw Castle in 1488, while in 1528 William Cunningham, 4th Earl of Glencairn, burned the Montgomery stronghold of Eglinton Castle, at Irvine.

Despite numerous attempts to broker a truce between the two families the internecine warfare continued, with Montgomerys and Cunninghams being killed in a series of tit-for-tat killings.

The slaying of a Cunningham by a Montgomery in 1584, apparently in self-defence, set off the tragic chain of events that led two years later to the murder of the young Earl of Eglinton.

The Cunninghams had immediately decided to exact vengeance for the killing of their kinsman.

A young man, Cunningham of Robertland was selected for the task and, accordingly, insinuated himself into a close friendship with the young Hugh Montgomery, who became earl on the death of his father in June of 1585.

In April of 1586, the earl, at the urging of his friend Cunningham of Robertland, accepted an invitation to dine at a house in the hostile Cunningham land of Lainshaw.

But, accompanied by only a few servants as he made his way back from the dinner, he was ambushed and killed by about 60 armed men, who included Cunningham of Robertland.

The vendetta dragged on, with countless numbers of Montgomerys and Cunninghams being slain or fleeing the country in fear of their lives.

It did not end until 1661, when William Cunningham, 9th Earl of Glencairn, married

Margaret Montgomery, daughter of the 6th Earl of Eglinton.

The tradition of medieval tournaments, meanwhile, recalling a glorious age of chivalry, was re-enacted in 1839 when the 13th Earl of Eglinton staged a famous tournament at the family's ancestral seat of Eglinton Castle.

Through marriage, the chiefs of the Montgomerys also hold, in addition to the earldom of Eglinton, the earldom of Winton, while the family motto is 'Watch well' and the crest is a woman holding an anchor in her right hand and the head of a savage in her left.

Chapter four:

Fame and acclaim

The Montgomerys continued their proud martial tradition in later centuries, most notably under Bernard Law Montgomery, 1st Viscount Montgomery of Alamein, who was descended from Montgomerys who had moved from Scotland to settle in Donegal, Ireland, in 1628.

Born in London in 1887, and affectionately known to his troops as 'Monty', Montgomery saw service with the British Army in India before serving with distinction during the First World War, when he was awarded the D.S.O for the gallant leadership of his men.

Appointed commander of the British Eighth Army in North Africa in August of 1942, he defeated the Axis forces of Germany and Italy at the battle of El Alamein in October of that year.

Knighted and promoted to general, he

later commanded the 21st Army Group, made up of the Allied ground forces that took part in the invasion of Normandy in June of 1944.

It was Montgomery who also accepted the surrender on May 4, 1945, of German forces in northern Germany, the Netherlands, and Denmark.

Created 1st Viscount Montgomery of Alamein in 1946, he later served as Chief of the Imperial General Staff. Often a rather outspoken and controversial figure in later life, he died in 1976.

In the world of literature, Alexander Montgomerie, born in Ayrshire about 1545, was a poet who served as poet laureate to the Scottish royal court.

Lucy Maud Montgomery, born on Prince Edward Island in 1874 and better known as L.M. Montgomery, was the Canadian author who wrote a series of novels that began in 1908 with *Anne of Green Gables* and ended in 1937 with *Jane of Lantern Hill*.

On the stage, Elizabeth Montgomery,

who was born in 1933 and died in 1999, was the American actress best known for her role as Samantha in the popular American comedy series *Bewitched*, that ran from 1964 until 1972, while Anthony T. Montgomery, born in Indianapolis in 1971, is the actor who has starred in the *Star Trek Enterprise* television series.

His grandfather, John Leslie Montgomery, better known as Wes Montgomery, was the highly talented American jazz guitarist who died in 1968.

In the world of sport, Jim Montgomery, born in Madison, Wisconsin, in 1955, is the American swimmer who, during the 1976 Montreal Olympics, became the first man to break the 50-second barrier in the 100 metres freestyle event.

On the golf course, Colin Montgomerie, born in Yorkshire in 1963 of Scottish parentage, is the popular golfer also referred to as 'Monty'.

His father, James, was the secretary of the Royal Troon Golf Club, and the young Montgomerie became one of the first British golfers to study at an American college, attending Houston Baptist University.

He first entered the top ten in the Official World Golf rankings in 1994, and at his peak was ranked as number two.

His career has been subject to various ups and downs, but in 2005 he returned to top ten ranking, the same year in which he became the first man to win 20 million Euros on the European Tour.

John Montgomery, born in Scotland in about 1750, immigrated to Virginia with his family and became a famed explorer.

He founded the city of Clarksville, Tennessee, and gave his name to Montgomery County, Tennessee.

Also in the United States, Montgomery, Alabama, was named after General Richard Montgomery, a renowned commander who was killed during the late eighteenth century American Revolutionary War.